THE SOUP DIET COOKBOOK

Lose Weight Naturally Without Hunger

Helen Cassidy Page

The Soup Diet Cookbook - Helen Cassidy Page. 1st edition
ISBN-13:978-1492181729
ISBN-10:1492181722

DEDICATION

I dedicate this book to my daughter, Allison Page, who is a model of healthy living and living with integrity and humor. She is my joy and my inspiration.

Table of Contents

Introduction 5

How To Get Rid Of Belly Fat 9

The Plan To Lose Belly Fat 13

Diet Truths...25

Don't Shoot The Messenger.........................27

How The Soup Diet Works 31

Soup Science...35

How To Use The Soup Diet 41

How Soon Will You See Results......................43

Sounds Too Good To Be True 47

Mix And Match Quick Start Plan 53

Eating Issues...55

Quick Start Diet 57

Portion Control..59

Quick Start Eating Plan 63

Quick Start Smoothie..................................67

Care And Feeding Of Your Soup Maker 69

Cooking, Weight Loss And Miscellaneous Tips 73

The Soups...81

Calories 83

Everyday Go-To Soup...................................85

Sweet Pea Soup With Mint 87

Carrot, Fennel and Blood Orange Soup 89

Creamy Vegetable Chowder.................................91

Spicy Cold Tomato Soup 93

Cream of Mushroom Soup 95

Zucchini and Garlic Soup................................97

Roasted Red Pepper Red Soup 99

Curried Carrot Soup 101

Roasted Cauliflower Soup 103

Cream of Eggplant and Tomato Soup 105

Spicy Asparagus Soup 107

Leek and Spinach Soup 109

Broccoli, Celery and Spinach Soup with Garlic.....111

Rutabaga and Carrot Soup 113

Roasted Red Beet and Orange Soup....................115

Lacinato Kale and Leek Soup............................117

Herbal Summer Squash Soup 119

Creamy, Lemony Spinach Soup 121

Cold Cucumber Herb Soup 123

Smoothies 125

Carrot, Apple, and Celery Smoothie 129

Blackberries, Apple, Blueberry Green Tea and Ginger
Smoothie..131

Grapes, Zucchini, Greens, and Celery Smoothie 133

Apple, Melon and Greens Smoothie....................135

Berries, Red Pepper, Celery, and Parsley Smoothie 137

Watermelon, Celery, Cucumber, and Greens Smoothie.......139

Grapefruit, Orange, Strawberry and Red Pepper Smoothie .141

Vegetable Juice, Celery, Apple, and Basil Smoothie.............143

Green Tea, Apple, Spinach, and Carrot Smoothie 145

Apple Cinnamon Smoothie 147

Give The Book A Thumbs Up 149

Medical Disclaimer 150

About Me 151

My Other Books................................152

Free Gift 153

Copyright Information 154

CHAPTER ONE

Introduction

Sigmund Freud asked that famous question, What do women want? He should have asked me. I know what we want. New clothes, live-in help, and a tiny jean size. Well, I'm afraid you're on your own for the first two, but The Soup Diet Cookbook can definitely help with the smaller waistline.

Everybody needs to watch their waistline these days, even those with relatively trim stomachs. Belly fat used to be a concern only when bikini season loomed. But now we know that, like shady used car loans, there are hidden costs to belly fat.

No one likes the sight of their muffin top spilling over his or her waistband. A substance called subcutaneous fat causes the muffin top. This fat sets up camp just under the skin and it is visible to the human eye (no matter how hard we try to hide it). Well, the fat isn't visible, just the unsightly bulge it causes. Subcutaneous fat makes it hard to zip and button and causes a reaction known as "suck it in, sister," whenever we pass a mirror. Most people think this is what we mean by belly fat.

But what's going on deep inside the belly is much worse. When the accumulation of fat uses up its storage space around the hips, thighs and belly, it has to go somewhere and it starts to wrap around the internal organs, known as the viscera. Gross, right? But so is the liver disease, heart disease, metabolic syndrome and a host of other problems caused by this visceral fat. We all have visceral fat and in healthy doses it pads the organs when we bounce around. Sort of like bubble wrap for the body. It is a good thing, except in excess.

Visceral fat doesn't just sit like sludge inside your body the way subcutaneous fat does. An over abundance of belly fat (it's medical name even though it may deposit itself away from the waistline), can cramp the organs the way two many bodies crush each other in an overcrowded subway train. Belly fat is metabolically active, meaning it releases compounds that can do serious damage to your body, causing problems such as high blood pressure, heart disease, and general poor health. One of the culprits in this devastating condition is visceral fat, or belly fat. And an ever-growing section of society is developing it.

Why are we having an epidemic of belly fat? Too much food and too much of the wrong food. Processed foods have not done our society any favors. Yes, they are convenient and sometimes tasty. But the price we pay for the additives, preservatives, artificial colors, over abundance of fat, sugar and sodium can be counted in obesity, high blood pressure and heart attacks. How to avoid belly fat? First step: no processed foods.

But if you are envying friends with no extra poundage and who have no trouble fitting into their clothes, slow down. They can be TOFI's. Thin on the outside, fat on the inside. And, no joke, TOFI is becoming a medical term. How can slim people have belly fat? Because so many of us are couch potatoes, or we sit at our computers and game consoles for hours on end when we should be spending some of that time exercising. We can burn off the calories we eat in our daily activities, but if we don't exercise and if we eat the wrong foods, this nasty visceral fat can accumulate without our realizing it.

And that is why belly fat is such a concern these days. It's not just about looking good in your clothes, though that's the benefit all the books and ads are pushing.

With the rates of overweight and obese people rising, there are more people at risk because of belly fat, the inner, visceral fat. It's double jeopardy when our weight gets out of control. The outer fat often makes us miserable because we don't like how we look, feel or how our clothes fit. But visceral fat may also be silently at work and we don't realize it until it has done some serious damage, until it is too late and we have a full blown heart attack or liver disease.

So as well as wanting to shed the fat in your upper arms, thighs, neck and wherever it accumulates for you, you are wise to buy this book and concern yourself with getting rid of dangerous belly fat. The Soup Diet Cookbook will help you do just that.

CHAPTER TWO

How To Get Rid Of Belly Fat

There are many ways to trick the body into shedding pounds without embarking on a full out regimented diet plan. Some of them are to eat 100 calories less a day. That can add up to ten pounds in a year. Eating more fiber, especially soluble fiber such as oat bran can reduce your calorie intake by 10-20 percent. And then of course, there is the soup approach. You can combine all of these methods to speed up weight loss. But without the soup, you don't get the hunger reduction benefit.

If you ever get sucked into watching late night TV, I mean REALLY late night TV, you will have no doubt come across infomercials for devices designed to melt away belly fat. Or pills, or some expensive plan that promises to transform you into a god or goddess with sleek, washboard abs.

Don't buy it. Literally. Step away from your credit card. The Soup Diet Cookbook will help you dissolve belly fat without spending any more of your hard earned cash.

Now a word about spot reducing, exercises that target a specific part of the body, such as the abs. It sounds good when you hear celebrity trainers pushing their program or device to give you a sleek stomach. Targeting your abdominal muscles with specific exercises or using some medieval torture device will not get rid of body fat without using diet and other measures. These methods may tone you. But research has shown that you must do cardiac exercise combined with a diet to dissolve body fat.

In The Soup Diet Cookbook you will discover the secret to losing between 28 and 42 pounds in a year without radically changing what you eat. Unlike the late night infomercials, this isn't pie in the sky, so to speak. This plan is based on sound science. Shortly you will read why The Soup Diet is so effective in helping you lose belly fat.

But diet won't do it alone. And so the Soup Diet Cookbook is a four pronged plan that will help you lose inner and outer fat in a very healthy, effective and medically sound way. The majority of this book will focus on the food plan. But first we are going to take a look at all the things you need to do to have the body you want, the health you need and the confidence you deserve from looking good and feeling even better.

CHAPTER THREE

The Plan To Lose Belly Fat

The Four Pronged Soup Diet Cookbook Plan To Finally And Permanently Lose Belly Fat

1. Exercise

Does anyone need convincing any more that we need to keep our bodies moving? And not just to maintain a fighting weight. Exercise helps keep blood pressure under control, keeps the heart strong, helps control diabetes, reduces stress and keeps you *lookin' good!* And, of course, it melts hidden belly fat.

Most of us don't need a pep talk on the *need* to exercise. The problem is getting over our *resistance* to exercise. Maybe this will help. New research shows that exercise makes us smarter. You don't have to be able to understand the science described in this article to get the bottom line: exercise improves brain function, as in our ability to solve tasks, and in brain structure. Is there anything exercise doesn't improve? So far we haven't found anything. Exercise is win-win no matter how you look at it.

What kind of exercise is best? Aerobic, hands down. Anything that gets your heart rate up and your lungs working harder. It doesn't have to be cross-country skiing or bicycling up a mountain. Walk faster than you normally do, for at least thirty minutes, even if it is just around the block. And as you get fitter, keep pushing the envelope. Walk a little faster and a little further. Go around the block twice. You get the picture.

And news flash: You don't have to join a gym, buy fancy work out clothes or hire a trainer. If you are old enough to read this book, and you don't have a physical disability, you know how to walk. So just get up and do it.

And if it's hard in the beginning and you find yourself huffing and puffing a lot, what can I say. That's why it's called exercise. But you will notice yourself increasing your endurance every week or ten days and that is a high in itself. I can tell you stories about people who couldn't make it to the first light pole when they started. In time they were running 5K races. So being tired and short of breath in the beginning is not a sign that you should stop. It is a sign that your body is right on target. Huffing and puffing a bit won't kill you (though it might feel like it). Belly fat and a sedentary lifestyle just might, though.

Get A Support System

If you lack the motivation to exercise on your own (don't feel guilty—many of us do), then if you can, by all means, join a gym and hire a trainer. More cost effective, though, is to meet up with your friends and walk the mall, run at lunchtime or bribe yourself into exercising.

Recent studies have shown that money is the best motivator to reach a goal. Tell a child you will give him a dollar to put the dishes in the dishwasher and that will get the kitchen cleaned far faster than threats or weekly checklists. And with less back talk!

If it works with a ten year old, yada, yada, yada. So partner with a pal and commit to an exercise program. Write up a schedule and share it with your buddy. Check in at the end of the week and if you skipped any of your sessions you have to contribute $10, $20, whatever amount you decide, to a New Shoes fund for your friend! Of course, while that would work for you as incentive to keep your hard earned cash by exercising, you might find your friend sabotaging your efforts to win the pot!

So, partner with a friend who also has exercise goals. You each put the money in a pot and at the end of six months the winner takes all. By winner, I don't mean the person who lost the most weight. I mean the person who missed the fewest exercise sessions. Studies show you can be healthier at a higher weight if you exercise, than at a lower weight if you don't. Remember TOFI?

Whatever method you use, commit to a MINIMUM of three 30-minute sessions of aerobic exercise each week. Then, in a short time, work up to adding resistance training twice a week, which can include yoga or Pilates, as well as weights. You can do more if so motivated, but those five sessions are the bottom line—three aerobic, two resistance. Your aerobics can be as simple as walking at a pace that makes conversation difficult up to and including marathon training. Resistance training can be as easy as using soup cans as weights while you do squats or pump up your arms. Watch the exercise channel or surf the net for workout videos.

It's up to you. *Just do it!* is a great slogan. But adding a cheering section makes it a lot easier and more fun.

Don't Ever Stop

And one other important thing about exercising. Bear in mind that this is a life-long program. You don't stop moving once you've reached your weight loss goals. Some of you may have read my other books where I talk about my recent heart surgery. My operation was not due to wayward lifestyle and eating habits, but because of a faulty heart valve. They run in my family.

Before I entered the hospital I met with my surgeon who has a very lighthearted demeanor. But at the end of the session he got very serious. When you recover, he warned me, you will exercise every day of your life. I don't want to see you becoming frail as you age and falling or breaking a hip after we go to all the trouble of fixing your heart. That happens because people don't stay strong by exercising. I don't care if you live to be 80, 90 or 100. You will run, walk, swim or bike. EVERY DAY OF YOUR LIFE. He actually snuck the F word in there for emphasis, which I won't repeat because this is a family cookbook.

So that's it, right from the horse's, or heart doctor's mouth. Start exercising and don't stop until you reach the pearly gates.

Exercise: Nothing Makes You Feel So Good

And think about this. We all can count up activities that make us regret them as a waste of time, from playing video games into the wee hours, to parking ourselves in front of the TV with a quart of ice cream, to flopping on the couch with a trashy book. Afterwards, we think, why did I do that? We've all done it.

But nobody ever says, after the pump and endorphin rush from an exercise session, I wish I hadn't done that. What a waste! I can't stand feeling this good!

2. Reduce Stress

The second component of The Soup Diet is to reduce stress. Many people pride themselves on the amount of stress they carry. As if juggling three cell phones, two computers, and texting during meetings is the path to inner peace. Stress can kill, simple as that. Stress can also make it very hard to lose weight. When we are stressed we release a chemical called ghrelin that causes us to experience hunger even when it isn't mealtime.

Stress also makes it easier to gain weight. When our adrenaline is racing and our anxiety levels climb, we turn to things that soothe us, like food.

Stress reduces our desire to engage in anything that involves discipline or deprivation, like a diet or exercise, no matter how necessary or healthful those activities may be.

It behooves us to reduce our stress load as much as possible. Easier said than done, right? Who has time? And how do you turn off the tapes in the brain that keep us anxious and tied up in knots.

Mindful Meditation

Well, I have a solution. It is called mindful meditation. Years ago meditation was considered a spiritual practice, not relevant if you weren't a Buddhist, for instance. Then brain scientists made some stunning discoveries about our neurons. Previously it was thought that we had a fixed number of brain cells, that our brain cells died as we aged. The brain never changed. Or as someone I know put it, aging led to stupidity. Oh, were we wrong. Subsequently, we learned that the brain is "plastic." That means it can grow and change. Now we know we can actually increase our IQ.

Many activities can improve our brain power. Among other things, scientists began looking at some remarkable claims by practitioners of meditation. They did studies, brain scans, the works. They found people who did a special kind of meditation called mindfulness or insight meditation, also known as vipassana, were calmer, happier, and healthier. Mindfulness meditation has become recognized as one of the most important things we can do for ourselves to promote physical, mental and emotional health. Even the U.S. military began training the troops in mindful meditation to help them cope with the stress of battle.

Meditation can be an important component of your healthy life plan to lose belly fat. You can take a class, read a book or join a meditation group. All these activities are good, and in fact, the more you do to learn this skill the better results you will have. But one of the easiest ways to learn meditation is to go online and find some tapes or a podcast. Sit in a comfortable chair, close your eyes and for five minutes, just follow the instructions.

You need only do it for five minutes at a time to get started, so this isn't a big time drain. It is easy. You can't do it wrong. And it will help you lose belly fat. My favorite meditation tapes are on iTunes U or found at:

http://marc.ucla.edu/body.cfm?id=22

You will find free podcasts on that site that will guide you through a session. Do it. It is fast, free and effective. If big, tough marines are doing it, what's your excuse?

3. Get Enough sleep

The third prong of The Soup Diet is sleep. You're thinking, seriously? Sleep? But you said get more exercise. How can I fit in more sleep? Don't you know I have a life?

Well, more and more studies are showing the harm we do to ourselves if we short circuit our nightly dose of zzzzzs. When it comes to weight loss, and in particular belly fat, the visceral fat that is so harmful in excess, a five-year study showed that participants who managed between a minimum of 6-7 hours sleep a night developed less visceral fat than those who managed only 5 hours or less.

And the nice thing about sleep? It feels so good when you do it.

When you follow the four-pronged Soup Diet, and exercise regularly and reduce stress, you may find it easier to get more and better sleep each night. If you are restless and have trouble falling asleep or you wake up in the night and then are dog tired in the morning after hours of tossing and turning, the combination of exercise, stress reduction and eating a healthier diet can be the answer to good, dreamy sleep, AND the loss of belly fat. What have you got to lose? Oh, yes. Belly fat.

4. Diet

This one is a no-brainer. To lose fat you must eat less. But for so many of us, cutting down on favorite foods is one of the hardest things we do. Well, suppose I told you that I have a secret to losing between 28-42 pounds a year. And suppose I showed that medical science has backed up this claim. Would you be willing to give it a try?

On top of that, suppose I told you that you didn't have to change your eating habits. No starvation diet, monotonously eating the same bland food every day, no giving up foods you love for foods you hate. Do I have your attention?

How badly do you want to lose weight and belly fat?

How much do you struggle with fad diets that leave you hungry, weak and ultimately poorly nourished, and then put the weight right back on?

Well pay attention, because I have the answer for you. It's soup.

Oh, no, you're saying, not that soup diet, where I eat a little bit of awful tasting soup three times a day and munch on toothpicks the rest of the time.

And no, that is not what I'm offering. Many people carry excess weight, not because they eat too much of bad food or have eating issues. We can enjoy a very healthy diet, but because we don't exercise enough or take too many extra helpings, the pounds creep on. For these people, I'm saying you can eat the same nourishing, delicious meals you enjoy now. But by adding some strategically designed recipes contained in this book, you will be able to embark on a weight loss program that is healthy, effective and easy. Keep reading and you will come to the specific plan for eating soup to lose weight. In addition, you will find a plan for boosting weight loss with The Soup Diet's Mix and Match plan. But first, . . .

CHAPTER FOUR

Diet Truths

All diets work if you stick to them.

No diet works if you give up on it.

To lose weight you must do two things:

- Eat less

- Exercise more (See Discussion No. 1 on Exercise above)

To lose weight we must burn more calories than we eat.

Weight doesn't fall off our hips over night. We must commit for the long haul.

Fad diets are unhealthy and keep you in an unhealthy relationship with food.

Fad diets that focus on one food or very low calories will not work because they are so restrictive you can't stick to them and they are so unhealthy they eventually make you feel ill.

Rapid weight loss is water not fat and returns as quickly as it came off

We overeat for many reasons. A diet is not going to change them.

Fad diets don't allow you to confront eating issues.

Studies show that a moderate calorie reduction diet is more effective in the long run than a quick fat-burner diet because people can stick to them. (That's a novel thought.)

The only way to keep your weight loss is to establish sound weight maintenance habits to last a lifetime.

You can make small changes that over time show big results.

CHAPTER FIVE

Don't Shoot The Messenger

If you don't like the list of diet truths you just read, don't blame me, blame your mother, Mother Nature, that is. She designed the human body to burn up a certain number of the calories for energy and to store the rest as fat. This worked when fat stores were essential for early man and woman. In those days they didn't have a fast food drive-in on the corner and might have to search for a while for some game or other goodies. Those fat stores saved them from starvation.

Since cave drawings don't show morbidly obese people, we can only assume that the calories in and calories out thing evened out over time and they didn't need Weight Watchers or the cabbage diet. My how times have changed.

I personally think that the problem of overeating and excessive weight gain is a very complex issue. It has less to do with self-control and more to do with living very complicated lives, in a very complicated world, with very complicated neurons, hormones and body chemistry running and sometimes thwarting our lives.

I personally believe that you have to be in a weight loss zone for a diet to work. How else to explain yoyo dieting? Good intentions get us to the program, but other things can sabotage us. Sometimes the program we choose is too restrictive and we just get too hungry. Sometimes a voice, a gremlin, or a part of ourselves we can't seem to control won't step up to the plate. Or maybe steps up to the plate too often. So to speak.

There is often a big gap between our desire to lose weight and our successful execution of a weight loss program. Sometimes, we just aren't ready. We have all the want in the world. We want to lose weight, we want to look better, we want to be healthier. The power of wanting those things can torture us, yet we can't make the necessary changes. We used to say that type of person had no discipline, that weight gain was a lack of character. These days we say we're not ready. But I suspect there is more to it. When are we not ready for a better life? But the answer to that problem is for another book, on the psychology and physiology of weight, eating, and motivation.

Still, when weight and unhealthy lifestyles are an issue, for our health and self-esteem, we must do all we can to control it. If you're tempted to envy those early people who could eat whatever they could get their hands on and fit into the same loin cloths year in and year out, ponder this. How good are you at out-running a saber-toothed tiger? Would you really like to live in a cave?

Whether we like it or not, we have to take what we've got, live in the world we live in with its temptations and stresses and be thankful medical science is taking weight control seriously.

Less and less we see the experts playing the blame game with weight. Instead they are recognizing that this weight and eating thing is a major problem in society. Constantly putting a guilt trip on those who struggle with it doesn't take a pound off anybody's hips. We can only cooperate the best we can with our determination to beat the beast. And look for a program that makes it easier.

What we can all do to deal with our weight and belly fat is find a program that works, that is healthy and that is not so extreme that we feel beaten up rather than slimmed down. And this is where The Soup Diet comes to the rescue.

No diet can give you the motivation to lose weight. That comes from within. But The Soup Diet can make the process more appealing when your inner self is ready to confront your outer self.

Special Eating Plans – The Soup Diet Is Paleo Friendly

You may follow a certain eating plan because it's medically recommended or it just makes you feel better. I don't consider them "fad" diets. Obviously, if you're diabetic, you will follow your medical caregiver's dietary recommendations. If you prefer to eat paleo, then a soup and smoothie regimen fits right in for you. There are only a few items you would avoid and they are options on the quick loss plan. The fats in the soup recipes coconut oil is listed as an option in all the recipes that call for a small amount of cooking fat. The remainder of the recipes fit in very well with a paleo eating plan.

CHAPTER SIX

How The Soup Diet Works

The Soup Diet works on soup science. That is, the physiology of the stomach and what we have learned about the chemicals that control hunger and satiety (that full feeling).

Studies show that people who eat half or a cup of soup before a meal, consume, on average, 135 fewer calories per meal, without making any other changes. They don't discard the mashed potatoes or the salad with blue cheese dressing. They just eat smaller portions because they are not as hungry. And they do this naturally. It just happens. They drink the soup, eat the soup, however you like to put it, and when they sit down to lunch or dinner half an hour later their stomach starts to shut down much sooner. They get that "I'm bursting at the seams" feeling while there is still food on their plate.

Yes, that means that if you were planning to have a meal of lamb chops with all the trimmings, you would not have to switch it to a salad with lemon juice for a dressing. You would find yourself eating less of that delicious meal because the soup would have already taken up some real estate in your stomach. When you eat less, you put yourself in the weight loss zone.

Can you imagine having that *I'm-bursting-at-the-seams-and-I'll-never-eat-another-meal* feeling when it isn't Thanksgiving?

Well, maybe you won't have the gut-busting food hangover that we look forward to at the holidays, but your tummy will just say, um, no thanks, to the next spoonful. I've had enough.

Do the math. By eating on average 135 fewer calories per meal, times three meals a day, you are cutting your intake by 405 calories a day. Multiply this by 365 days in a year and you have cut out 147,825 calories in a year. At 3,500 calories in a pound of fat, that translates to approximately a 42-pound weight loss in a year. Naturally, these results will vary from person to person, but studies published in The American Journal of Clinical Nutrition and conducted in major universities have backed up these results.

If you skip soup at breakfast and go for a bigger start to your day, with soup at two meals you are looking at approximately a 28-pound weight loss in a year. While you are eating your usual foods.

You won't have to eat a cabbage leaf every meal and gnaw on toothpicks in between. You can enjoy real food, every day at every meal. This is true because scientific studies have shown that the body has its own secret weight loss switch, and it is triggered by eating soup.

Wouldn't you like to control hunger pangs so you could stick to a diet? Wouldn't you like to lose up to 42 pounds a year and still enjoy the meals you already eat?

Then eat soup. Not just any soup. The soups in The Soup Diet Cookbook. A particular type of soup sets up complex processes in the stomach and brain to keep hunger at bay longer than other foods, and helps you resist messages to eat more than you need. Now let's look at the science.

CHAPTER SEVEN

Soup Science

Lest you think I'm making this up, scientists have looked into the stomach to get a better understanding of our number one health problem, obesity. Literally looked into, with ultrasound and MRI scans. They observed first hand this good thing that happens with soup.

They had already discovered in the late 1990's the chemical ghrelin that, when the stomach is empty, sends a message to the brain asking for more food. It may not be mealtime, we may not actually need food. But once ghrelin is on the move, I dare you to think about anything else besides food.

Gremlin has picked up the moniker, the Hunger Hormone. Fasting, for example, floods the brain with ghrelin, essentially keeping us begging for food.

Without ghrelin signaling us to eat, perhaps we'd starve. But when too much ghrelin flows into our system, we are always asking for more food, too much food.

What triggers a ghrelin overload besides actual hunger? Stress. Yes, the knots in your stomach because you aren't going to meet the work deadline, the headache because the paycheck isn't stretching as far as it needs to, the ache in your heart because the loved one is sick or you just have too much on your plate and not enough time or money or inner strength to cope with it all. That's the stress I'm talking about, the stress we all have that contributes to the production of ghrelin.

Now you understand why I have made a point of including stress reduction as part of The Soup Diet. Reducing the production of ghrelin is one of the goals of stress reduction programs. Which is why I urge you start meditating every day, just five minutes to start. Here below is the link to free podcasts, though there are many books, classes and tapes that will teach you this simple method of getting centered and more peaceful in your life. And reining in ghrelin. Just paste this link into your browser:

http://marc.ucla.edu/body.cfm?id=22

Hunger Is Bad For You, And It Doesn't Feel Good

Scientists believe that complex interactions between chemicals, adaptations by our early ancestors, and today's eating patterns and the abundance of easily available food contribute to our obesity rates.

If I were to ask you what the biggest stumbling block to dieting is for you, chances are high that you would say, hunger. If you didn't have your mind on food all the time because you were so hungry, you might have better success. Well scientists are looking at that.

We are now learning that it is not useful to maintain a state of hunger, such as that on very low calorie diets, if we want to lose weight. That gremlin ghrelin won't let us keep our mind off food. But if we keep the stomach full, the ghrelin gremlin calms down and leaves us alone. As long as we feel full, we can concentrate on other things. Well, aren't we going around in circles here? How do we stop feeling hungry without eating more?

Here's where The Soup Diet comes in. Science has also pinpointed a mechanism in our body that can help control hunger, and it is activated by soup. Scientists have learned that a combination of food mixed with water helps this process. However, a forkful of chicken and a drink of water won't accomplish this because the water or liquid empties out of the stomach quickly.

But if you mix food and liquid into a soup, specifically a pureed soup, something called the pyloric sphincter valve at the end of the stomach shuts the door on the stomach for a while. This puree or slurry of food and liquid prevents the stomach from emptying out completely, the way it does with other foods. Hence, the digestive juices can go to work on the food trapped in the stomach. With food in our stomach, we have no hunger. No hunger, no ghrelin. And this is how we can curb hunger without eating more food.

All this from soup. This explains why low calorie diets don't work and why The Soup Diet recommends pureed soups half an hour before a meal, and then eating a real meal. The digestive process has already started by the time you sit down to your meal. Your stomach is slightly full and you desire less of your dinner, or lunch or snack.

And speaking of snacks, eating pureed soup between meals curbs hunger for much longer, keeping ghrelin at bay and you on target.

The Soup Diet Cookbook contains twenty low calorie, pureed vegetable soups and ten smoothies, which are basically cold soups, to trick your body into cooperating with your efforts to get back into your skinny jeans and dissolving that harmful belly fat.

So there we have the 4-pronged plan in The Soup Diet.

1. Exercise

2. Reduce Stress

3. Get More sleep

4. Eat Soup

You must commit to all four of these fat-reducing steps. To lose belly fat, you must exercise to work off excess calories, get enough sleep to help the body control weight and reduce stress through meditation to slow down the production of ghrelin and help create a calmer, fuller, thinner you.

CHAPTER EIGHT

How To Use The Soup Diet

The soup diet could not be easier to follow. Approximately one-half hour before a scheduled meal, consume one-half to one cup of the soup or smoothies in this cookbook. That's all. No other special meal planning is involved, unless you want to rev up your weight loss with the Mix and Match Weight Loss Plan that follows.

It is important that you keep these soups on hand. I believe in making life easy as possible. Prepare several batches in different flavor combinations and freeze them in small batches so you can just stick them in the microwave when you need them.

Or, you can whip up a smoothie for the same results. I've even frozen left over smoothies and allowed them to defrost on the counter. Whirl them in the blender and you're good to go.

CHAPTER NINE

How Soon Will You See Results

The soup diet could not be easier to follow. Approximately one-half hour before a scheduled meal, consume one-half to one cup of the soup or smoothies in this cookbook. That's all. No other special meal planning is involved, unless you want to rev up your weight loss with the Mix and Match Weight Loss Plan that follows.

It is important that you keep these soups on hand. I believe in making life easy as possible. Prepare several batches in different flavor combinations and freeze them in small batches so you can just stick them in the microwave when you need them.

Or, you can whip up a smoothie for the same results. I've even frozen left over smoothies and allowed them to defrost on the counter. Whirl them in the blender and you're good to go.

How Soon Will You See Results?

I know you would like me to say you will have lost your belly fat in two or three days, but you wouldn't believe me if I did. At least I hope you wouldn't. Weight gain doesn't happen overnight (though it seems that way), and it isn't going to go away overnight (I can hear you saying, *you got that right*).

But the fat will go away. By consuming less food, you burn more calories. So there will be results. It's a law of physics.

Weight loss on The Soup Diet averages 3.5 pounds a month. Slow and steady wins the race, but for many that is too slow. If you choose to cut down even further on your normal meals, you will lose weight faster, but it is not necessary.

By losing weight more slowing and letting your body and psyche adjust to the changes, there is a greater chance that the weight loss will be permanent. You will be establishing new habits that can stick.

However, if you have a great deal of weight to lose and your health is at stake so much so that you need to lose weight faster, then choose the Mix and Match Weight Loss Plan that follows.

What Kind Of Dieter Are You?

There are two kinds of dieters. First are those who want instant gratification. If asked, I'd bet that is most of us, but I haven't done a scientific study. Next are those who can't stand pain. They are happy to go a slower route to avoid the deprivation in most diets. They can wait awhile for the results to show while making just a few changes in their diet and lifestyle. They trust the process.

Choose The Mix and Match Quick Start Plan For Instant Gratification

The Mix and Match Quick Start Plan is for the Instant Gratification gang, those who want a head start on losing a few pounds. Mix and Match takes the fretting and planning out of weight loss. You will eat the soup or smoothie before each meal. But, in addition, you will eat a leaner meal in order to speed up calorie burning.

This plan gives you five options for your main dishes, and several suggestions for low calorie, low fat sides. This plan is based on a section of The Stanford Healthy Heart Cookbook and Lifeplan, which I wrote with Dr. John Schroeder and Tara Dickson, R.D.

CHAPTER TEN

Sounds Too Good To Be True

If weight loss were fun and easy, we wouldn't have an obesity problem in this country. I would be lying if I said The Soup Diet doesn't involve any cooperation on your part.

If, instead of The Mix and Match Plan, you choose to eat your normal meals, but with reduced portions, you must do one very import thing. This is crucial and I cannot stress it strongly enough. You must become hyper aware at mealtime.

So many of us are mindless eaters. If it's in front of us, we eat until it is all gone. You can read an excellent book by Brian Wasink, a food scientist at Cornell University, on this subject. His book is available on his website.

It is fun and eye opening. The takeaway is that we don't pay attention to what we put in our mouth. Often it is gone before we know we've eaten a meal. You are not alone in this habit, but it is hard to break.

If you don't pay attention to what you are eating and the signals from your stomach that you are full, you will simply be adding calories to your meal, delicious, healthful ones, but more calories nonetheless. There is a lag time between the food enters our mouth and the brain responds with a message to stop eating. We have to learn to recognize that signal, give ourselves time for the signal to get through.

If we eat too quickly, or mindlessly, and don't pay attention to what is left on our plate instead of how our stomach feels, we will always eat too much. The impulse is to finish our dinner. Wasn't that how we were trained? Eat everything on your plate, or else.

That was fine when we were growing and our active bodies burned off the calories. But as adults, with more sedentary lives and many distractions at mealtime, we can finish a meal before we realize we have taken a bite. We get caught up in conversations or, if we are alone, we may watch television or read while we eat. We assume that if there is food in front of us, we have to eat it, no matter how full our stomach feels.

Many people are surprised when they start The Soup Diet to realize what a sense of fullness feels like, and what it is like to discover they don't need any more food.

But this is all you have to do. Stop being a mindless eater if that is your habit. Eat your soup. Let it get the digestive process going. Enjoy your meal and stop eating as soon as you realize you are full.

Notice I didn't say pass on the gravy or the salad dressing you love. Eat those foods, but with the help of the low calorie soup before the meal, you will desire smaller portions. On average, about 20% less.

One reason people like The Mix and Match Quick Loss Plan is that you don't have to think about how much you are eating. The portion control is built into the plan and troublesome foods are eliminated.

But you can feel deprived, especially at first. You have to employ awareness and commitment to stay with the plan. That is true of any diet and don't let anyone tell you any different.

The beauty of The Soup Diet Plan is that when you feel hungry, reach for soup. It is low calorie PLUS it helps get the hunger pangs under control. Am I promising that you will never feel hunger or discomfort associated with cutting down your calorie intake? No, it's just that it is so much easier to manage with The Soup Diet.

If you choose to eat your usual meals, rather than The Mix and Match Plan, you must be aware of what you are eating. Pay attention to the sensation of fullness and stop when you reach it. It is not hard for us to push through a feeling of fullness and keep eating more than we need to because we simply are not paying attention to our body, but to what is on the plate. If there is food on the plate, we think the law of the universe demands that we finish it.

In time you will learn to prepare smaller portions so you don't waste food if your reach a comfortable state of fullness and have to stop before you have finished your meal. Keep in mind that leftovers are great!

Now remember my encouragement to start a mindfulness meditation practice? This will help you become aware of your body sensations and make it easier to recognize when you are full. Score one for the meditation team.

I am not suggesting that you have to leave the table uncomfortably hungry. You just have to recognize when you are full, and stop. This may be the hard part for you, not hunger, but to get out of the loop of habitual eating, because just like Mt. Everest, it is there. You have to pay attention to what is going on in your belly, for a leaner belly.

CHAPTER ELEVEN

Mix And Match Quick Start Plan

This plan will cut your calories so that you lose weight faster. But you may not enjoy the same sensation of fullness as you would eating soup and then eating a normal but smaller meal. You must keep in mind your motivation. Do you need to get rid of 10 or 15 pounds for a special occasion or just for your mental health? Then this plan will do it, but there is a tradeoff. You will have to restrict your portions whether you feel full or not. You may have to say goodbye for a while to foods you love.

Keep in mind that you can always enjoy a cup of soup to stem hunger pangs between meals. And keep in mind the long-term goal, of a slimmer and healthier you.

Stick to The Mix and Match Plan for a month and then go back to soup plus your normal meals. If you have a lot of weight to lose, and your health is at issue because of it, consult with a health care professional before starting The

Soup Diet. Share it with your physician or nutritionist and use it to design a plan that suits your health needs. Whatever plan you choose, even one that is different from the two mentioned in this book, the soups and smoothies are low calorie, virtually fat-free and full of nutrition. They will fit into any meal plan and give you the same hunger-curbing results.

As I end this section, I want to remind you that in one sense, all weight loss plans are the same, they push fewer calories in, and more energy out in the form of exercise. Until we find a way around physics, all diets have that in common.

But not all diets are the same in terms of offering you a healthy, well-balanced meal plan, or one that will help you control hunger and cravings.

CHAPTER TWELVE

Eating Issues

If you are someone with eating issues, you need to keep a few things in mind.

A diet doesn't cure food issues. Conflicts with food have less to do with what you weigh and the food you eat than the reasons you crave food. This book will not resolve them, though I wish it could.

Seek as much support as you can, from professionals, support groups, friends and family before, during and after you embark on The Soup Diet. Those who struggle with food issues often find it is a life-long process.

The most important thing you can do, whether or not food is a struggle for you, is to eat a healthy diet. Fad diets that severely limit calories by restricting the types of food you eat keep you in a negative relationship with food. You feel you are trying to beat down the beast, when you need to make peace with food. You want to enjoy your food, even if you have to avoid something you love, such as tubs of ice cream.

So much research is being done on food issues, from compulsive eating, bingeing, and anorexia to negative body image. Seek as much help as is available and you can afford. There are low or no cost support groups that can be invaluable. Don't give up. Don't let lapses trick you into believing you can't do it. You've heard this before, but no one is perfect. To err is human. Failing is not what matters, but that you pick yourself up and try again. It is the only way any of us succeed at anything.

CHAPTER THIRTEEN

Quick Start Diet

Following The Soup Diet can lead to an average 42 pound weight loss over a year's time, or about 3.5 pounds a month. While that is a healthy weight loss, you may want to rev up your diet goals and have some instant gratification at the beginning. For that purpose, The Mix and Match Quick Start Weight Loss Diet is the perfect program to help you lose more weight quickly in the beginning without starving yourself and, while still keeping your meal plan healthy.

Here's how it works.

Continue to have one-half to one cup of soup or smoothie approximately thirty minutes before mealtime.

For breakfast, choose one of the suggested protein options, and two of the optional sides.

For lunch, do the same thing. Choose one protein and then add the optional items.

For dinner, choose a protein main course from those suggested and two or three of the optional items.

Every day be sure you eat 5 portions of fruit and 9 portions of vegetables. The anti-oxidant-laden fruit and vegetable soups and smoothies will help you reach that number. At every meal, season your food with your favorite low calorie, low sodium condiments to add pizazz and interest to your meals.

CHAPTER FOURTEEN

Portion Control

Portion control is essential to achieving any weight loss goal. A range of recommended daily calorie targets on The Mix and Match Quick Start Plan will range from 1,300-1,800 for women to 1,500 to 2,000 or 2,500 for men. Exact daily targets to maximize weight loss will depend on whether you are a man or a woman and how active or sedentary you are.

For this reason, I don't list exact portions or serving sizes because they can vary for each person. A 6'4" active man who starts a gym program along with The Soup Diet Plan will need at least 1,500-1,700 calories. A 3-ounce portion of fish at dinner may not give him the protein he needs. Whereas, a 135 pound woman who is 5'4" and just wants to loose ten pounds, but is not active, may do fine on a 3-ounce portion of chicken breast. Instead of exact portion sizes, I recommend you look up your BMI on one of the recommended websites below and use that as your calorie guide.

A Body Mass Index or BMI reading, will help you determine your healthy weight goals and the calories you need to consume to reach and maintain that target. I recommend you check out a site such as Buddy Slim, or a weight control site of your choosing. They offer special calculators that determine your BMI from your height and weight.

In the long run you will be far more successful if you discover what is right for your body, than trying to fit yourself into a calorie count that does not meet your body's needs. What matters is that you eat less and exercise more. What is more important is that you have a means of controlling the hunger that trashes so many efforts to lose weight. And that is what you will find in The Soup Diet.

Portion control is largely a concern on the Mix and Match Quick Start Plan because you want to accelerate your weight loss. Consequently, portion size and eliminating high calorie foods are what counts. But by choosing the meal plan that follows, you will have eliminated those diet dangerous foods.

If you choose to have a cup of soup or a smoothie half an hour before your normal meal and stop eating when your stomach signals it is full, then you don't have to worry about portion sizes or calorie counts. Naturally, you have to be honest with yourself and make sure you are not merely adding the drinks to your meal, but allowing them to help you eat less, naturally. If you drink the soup and then eat as much as you normally would, of course your weight won't budge.

Be aware that you may not feel full immediately upon drinking your soup or smoothie and think this plan is not working. Remember that it takes about 15 or 20 minutes for the fullness in your stomach to signal the brain that it is full, and then for the brain to tell you stop eating. By that time, you may have over eaten. So slow down and it will be easier to recognize when you've had enough.

But by the time you make it to the table 30 minutes later for your regular meal, your stomach will have filled sufficiently for you to naturally desire less food. And that sense of fullness will last for hours after you have eaten.

All that said, I do list typical portion sizes for the following suggested meals, and leave it up to you to be honest about your intake.

CHAPTER FIFTEEN

Quick Start Eating Plan

The Mix and Match Quick Loss Eating Plan

Breakfast: Choose one:

- Whole egg, boiled, poached, scrambled or fried with 1 teaspoon yogurt butter or coconut oil

- 3 ounces cooked skinless, boneless chicken or turkey breast, canned tuna or salmon, packed in water and drained

- 1 low fat chicken sausage

- ½ cup whole grain cooked cereal with ½ cup skim milk

- 8 ounces Mix and Match Protein Smoothie (recipe follows)

- 1 cup fat-free cottage cheese

- 1 cup Greek low-fat yogurt

Optional Sides: Choose 2

- 1 cup fresh fruit: berries, apple, stone summer fruits, pear

- 1 tablespoon fat-free, sugar-free fruit spread

- 1 ounce low fat cheese

- ½ whole grain bagel or equivalent bread, waffle, or pancake

Lunch: Choose one:

- ½ cup chicken salad with fat-free mayonnaise, apples and celery

- 3 ounces cooked skinless, boneless chicken or turkey breast, canned tuna or salmon

- 1 hard boiled egg, stuffed with 1 tablespoon low-fat mayonnaise, pinch of curry powder and tablespoon Major Gray's Chutney

- 1 cup low-fat cottage cheese

- 1 cup low-fat yogurt

- 2 cups green salad with 3 ounces very lean roast beef, trimmed of all fat and 2 ounces walnuts and low fat dressing

- Middle Eastern plate of hummus, tabouli, Baba Ghanouj, 2 ounces very lean lamb trimmed of all fat

Optional sides: Choose two:

- 1 cup fresh fruit: berries, apple, stone summer fruits, pear

- ½ cup tropical fruit, such as pineapple, mango or papaya

- 2 cups green salad with 1 tablespoon vegetable oil-based dressing

- 1 whole grain roll or small whole grain muffin

Dinner: Choose one:

- 3 ounces grilled, baked or poached fish such as salmon, sea bass, tilapia, mahi mahi

- 1 cup low or nonfat chili, choose from black bean, vegetarian or turkey

- 1 cup cooked lentils with 1 cup cooked quinoa

- ½ cup pasta with tomato meat sauce

- Steamed or roasted vegetable salad with 1 cup garbanzo or white beans

- Egg white frittata with vegetables and 2 heaping tablespoons coarsely grated Parmesan cheese

- Red beans and Rice

Optional sides, choose 2:

- 12 small to medium frozen sweet potato fries

- 4 cups greens in salad with 1 tablespoon olive oil-based dressing

- 1 whole grain roll

- ½ avocado

CHAPTER SIXTEEN

Quick Start Smoothie

This smoothie is a meal in itself. Low in fat, dense with calcium and high on flavor.

1 cup 1% milk
1 cup nonfat Greek yogurt
¼ cup protein powder, flavor of your choice
1/3 cup nonfat dry milk powder
½ cup berries, peach, plum, nectarine or banana
3 or 4 ice cubes

Place all ingredients in a blender jar and puree until smooth.

Servings: 1

CHAPTER SEVENTEEN

Care And Feeding Of Your Soup Maker

The appliance you use to puree your soups and smoothies will become your best friend as you embark upon The Soup Diet. If you purchase a blender, immersion blender, juicer or food processor for this purpose you will have made an investment in your health and added greatly to the convenience of mealtime.

Here are some tips for caring for your appliance so it will give you years of service and ensure that you use it safely.

Make sure that you keep all parts of the appliance that come in contact with food squeaky clean. Bacteria can set up housekeeping in an unwashed blender jar that sits on the counter for a while. If you use it before washing it out thoroughly, giving it only a quick pass under cold water, you are asking for trouble.

Most blender jars and food processor bowls are dishwasher safe. Follow the manufacturer's instructions for assembling and taking apart the jars, lids and blades and wash and dry each component thoroughly after use.

The blades for immersion blenders usually are dishwasher safe. However, keep the handle dry, as that is where the motor is and dunking it in water will ruin it.

Standalone juicers strain the pulp out of fruits and vegetables and produce clear, delicious juices. While these juices are full of good nutrition to say nothing of flavor, consume them in addition to the smoothies. A clear juice won't delay hunger the way a smoothie will and you don't get all that good fiber.

"Juicer" juices are always a healthy and delicious way to get plant nutrients. However, the Soup Diet aims to keep a soupy consistency remaining in the stomach long enough to prolong digestion and keep the ghrelin gremlins at bay. This is what will keep you feeling full and satisfied longer. Puree these clear juices with melon or greens to create a pulpy drink. Clear juices will not sabotage The Soup Diet, and if you want to use only your juicer, you will be getting excellent nutrition. However, they won't keep you feeling full for as long as thicker smoothies.

Dealing with the pulp in these machines probably deters many users from juicing on a regular basis. It is my unprofessional guess that many juicing resolutions go by the wayside because juicers are such a pain to clean. More than any other appliance, I think, the juicer spends most of its life in the back of a cupboard. If you use this type of juicer, get in the habit of cleaning it as soon as you use it. As the pulp dries, it becomes harder to clean.

If your juicer, blender or food processor sits for awhile before washing and dried-on pulp accumulates, mix a solution of 2 tablespoons baking soda and 2 tablespoons cold water and whirl it in your appliance for 30 seconds or so. Then wash as usual and you should find the dried bits loosened.

Wash all of the extra parts thoroughly and make sure they're dry before reassembling. Be sure your machine is dry before using it again.

Store your machine, whether on the counter or in the cupboard, with all the parts assembled so you don't lose any. They can be a nuisance to replace.

For blenders, add liquid or softer items at first and then when they are partially blended, stop the machine and add the other ingredients. This is also easier on the motor as it doesn't have to work as hard to pulverize the solids and ice if you are using it in smoothies.

Always follow these safety tips:

Do not uncover a machine while it is running, especially if it is pureeing hot liquids. The contents will spray and likely burn you.

Do not start the machine until the cover is securely tightened.

Hold the lid down with a kitchen towel---just in case.

Start the machine on the slowest speed and work your way up to the pureeing speed.

Do not use items the manufacturer states will harm the machine. Unless you own a Blendtec, don't put your iPhone in the blender jar!

CHAPTER EIGHTEEN

Cooking, Weight Loss And Miscellaneous Tips

Essentials

Whether you follow the Mix and Match Plan or eat your usual meals, it is important to include a tablespoon of vegetable oil every day for optimum health. While olive oil can be the oil of choice in many recipes, you need linoleic acid every day, which is only found in oils such as canola.

It cannot be repeated often enough, fruits and vegetables are the key to good health. One of the side benefits of The Soup Diet Plan is that the soups and smoothies go a long way to meeting that requirement.

Other Weight Loss Tips

There are several foods and habits that can whittle away belly fat without resorting to a restricted diet. Eating pureed soup is only one of them, but the most powerful in reducing hunger and allowing you to eat the foods you love. Here are some other tips to try:

Reduce your calorie intake by 100 calories a day. That could be a pat of butter on your toast, a smaller portion of meat or cutting out one snack. These small changes can add up to a 10-pound loss in a year.

Eat more fiber. Add 15 grams of fiber a day and you can strip as much as 10% from your calorie intake.

Snack on nuts, particularly walnuts and pinenuts. They go a long way to curbing hunger. A small handful will do it. If you go overboard, of course, the fat in nuts will add too many calories, overriding the hunger reducing benefits. A small handful, 2-3 tablespoons is a reasonable portion.

Many people swear by consuming a tablespoon of apple cider vinegar a day in a glass of water. It's tough love in my book, but research seems to show it is effective. Sometimes we need all the help we can get, no matter how bitter the medicine. On the other hand, if you jones on vinegar, this may just be the tip for you.

You can also try the feel-good trick of a piece of dark chocolate. Endorphin producing, dark—not milk, can cut appetite cravings. Of course, if chocolate is a trigger food for you where one bite is too much and a pound isn't enough, pass on to the next tip of tricking yourself by putting your food on a small plate. Dr. Wasink, mentioned above, discovered that meals served on large and small plates were perceived differently. Put a meal on a large plate with room around the edges and the diner goes away hungry. Put the same meal on a small plate where the gravy is dripping over the side, and the same diner goes away full. So much in life is perception. Make it work for you by serving meals on smaller lunch or salad plates rather than large dinner.

Can You Use Store-Bought Commercial Soups?

The only caveat for soup and smoothies is that they must contain low calorie fruits, vegetables, plus liquid and be pureed. The recipes in this cookbook are designed for maximum flavor. However, they do not contain items that are high in calories or sodium that you might find in regular soup cookbooks. They contain no cheese, pasta, potatoes, cream or milk. The smoothies also use low calorie fruits and vegetables, but no bananas, protein powder, yogurt or milk. These things are not bad or forbidden, but the goal is weight loss and it is best for the duration of the diet that you do not include them in your soups and smoothies as they are too high in calories. If you choose to eat these foods, then include them as part of your regular meal plan, not added on in the soups and smoothies.

If it is not convenient to make these recipes from scratch, then yes, of course you can purchase soups and smoothies, but with this reservation. They must be very low in calories and they must be pureed, not chunky. Don't choose soups with any additives or preservatives or high calorie ingredients.

You don't have to dash your diet hopes because you don't have time to prepare any of these soups. But for the maximum weight loss, use these or similar recipes as often as possible. The collection of soups in The Soup Diet Cookbook are more varied than any you will find on your supermarket shelves or take out counter. The more interesting and delicious the soup, the more likely you are to grab a cupful, zap it in the microwave and set yourself up for a lower calorie meal.

The recipes are easy to make. Because of the limitations of the types of soups you can eat, the recipes and techniques are similar, though because of the variety of vegetables used, the flavors are quite different.

Many of these creamy soups will have you believing they contain real cream. That is the idea behind these recipes: to make them as appealing and delicious as possible. You can choose your favorites and make them over and over or try every one in the book. By then, you will no doubt be coming up with your own fruit and vegetable combinations.

But if you can't do that, head for your favorite market. Many take out soups will fill the bill, but ask for the ingredient list. Several box soups are also creamy without being highly caloric.

When To Eat The Soup

About 30 minutes before a meal, make a smoothie or heat up a portion of soup, between one-half cup to one cup. Then have your usual meal, but pay attention to your sensation of fullness. If you are prone to mindless eating, where you keep going until the only thing left on the plate is the label on the bottom, then stop after every few bites to check your state of hunger. One of the pluses of The Soup Diet is that you train yourself to recognize hunger signals so you can stop eating when you have had enough. After half an hour or so, have your regular meal or The Mix and Match Quick Start selection.

Cooking Tips

Fresh vs. Dried Herbs

Let's face it, these are simple soups. Which is not to say that they aren't full of flavor and nourishment. The goal, though, is to create low calorie, pureed soups that will stay in the stomach longer to stave off hunger and help you lose weight. What distinguishes this collection of soups is the mix of flavors achieved by blending various, complementary flavors for a unique taste sensation with each recipe. Because we can't use cream, butter, flavorful oils, cheese, potatoes, pastas, and proteins such as chicken or beans, as you would for a typical soup, the key to achieving tasty soups that suit this particular purpose, is to use herbs and seasonings that increase flavor without adding calories. When a recipe calls for fresh herbs, always add them at the end. This keeps their flavor bright and fresh because cooking dulls the taste of fresh herbs. If you use dried herbs, however, you may add them at the beginning of the soup, for instance when you add the liquid. For more information on how to use (and even grow) fresh herbs, check out Jackie Johnson's book, Twelve Best Herbs For Flavor.

Butter Substitutes

While you can make life easier for yourself by putting all the ingredients in a soup pot and boiling them together, you will get more flavor with this simple, low calorie trick. I use a small quantity of yogurt butter as a butter substitute, about a teaspoon, which has about 13 calories, mixed with a bit of stock to sauté onions and garlic before adding the vegetables and liquid to the soup. This technique mimics sautéing well enough so that you get the softened, slightly caramelized hints without flooding your soup with high calorie oil.

You can use any brand of yogurt butter, but my personal favorite is Brummel and Brown, available in many stores, although there are others. These blends contain real butter and is a better cooking substitute in small quantities than the usual butter substitutes. I find that it melts more like real butter, whereas other butter substitutes just sit in the bottom of the pan. They are good for spreads, less so for cooking. I use yogurt butter on my toast every morning and in many dishes calling for butter. If you can't locate it, use another butter substitute or real butter. The quantity is so small you won't do serious damage to your diet, but every calorie counts.

NOTE: Since first publishing this book several readers have notified me that they are unable to locate the yogurt butter I recommend. There are several substitutions on the market that use a small amount of butter, but if you can't find one, use all oil.

When sautéing onions, garlic, leeks or shallots in such a small amount of fat, add a generous pinch of salt. It draws the liquid out of the vegetables and there is less chance of scorching.

Coconut Oil

For paleo eating plans, substitute coconut oil 1-1 for other fats.

Stocks and Broths

I use mostly chicken stock because it has more flavor. When I have the time, I make it myself. Other times I use boxed or canned without preservatives. Should you use low-sodium? That's always a good idea in the salt-laden food world we live in. However, low-sodium stocks do not have as much flavor as the regular version. Use your judgment. If you have been advised to keep your salt/sodium intake down (they are not the same: salt is in a shaker, sodium is hidden in many foods), then by all means use low sodium stocks and broths.

If you are a vegetarian or vegan, simply substitute vegetable stock or water where the recipe calls for chicken or beef. With the exception of stock, these recipes are meat and dairy free.

CHAPTER NINETEEN

The Soups

Here they are now. A collection of delicious, healthy, colorful soups that are easy to prepare and will help you combat the hunger pangs that sabotage so many efforts to eat healthier and lighter.

For the most part these recipes call for fresh vegetables. However, so many food manufacturers offer frozen vegetables without salt, butter or additives that you can use these convenience foods freely in these recipes. You will have the same nutritional boost that you would get from fresh, with only a slight decrease in flavor. If you have your own garden patch or can frequent a farmer's market, then using just-picked veggies will send these soups over the top.

You can count these soups as part of your daily produce requirement. You can freeze and save leftovers in small containers for another time.

If these soups seem repetitive, just vegetables pureed with stock or water, remember this is not all you will eat. Unlike other soup diets that prescribe a watery soup three times a day and chewing on your knuckles in between, you will consume these low calories soups in addition to your meal.

Additionally, you can enjoy them as snacks and whenever you feel hungry during the day. They do not contain starchy vegetables, pastas, cheese or dairy products, which keeps them lean. If you add any of these items to your soups, count them toward your mealtime calorie consumption.

A word about The Everyday Go-To Soup. You may at times want something you can chew on, so to speak, for a change of pace. This soup has the same calorie range as the other soups and you can eat it during the day to fend off hunger. It doesn't provide quite the same hunger-reducing power as the pureed soup, but it is still a valuable soup to have in your arsenal. When you come home from the market with a selection of fresh fruits and vegetables, you may want to taste the distinctive flavors in a soup. Here's the recipe you need.

CHAPTER TWENTY

Calories

I don't list calorie counts for the soups because they are all so low that a few calories one way or another will not matter in the daily scheme of things. A serving will be between 50 and 100 calories, depending on whether you consume the entire portion or split it up into two or more portions. Some soups make two or more servings, as indicated, so that you can save or freeze some for convenience sake.

I think that's it for soup science. Now for the recipes, always the best part of any cookbook.

And remember: Any diet works if you stick to it! Bon Appetit.

CHAPTER TWENTY-ONE

Everyday Go-To Soup

This is the soup you will have on hand at all times in the freezer or refrigerator. It is so low in calories that you can have a cup anytime hunger threatens your resolve to stick to the Mix and Match Quick Loss plan. Not developed as a before a meal soup because it is not pureed, which gives you the edge on hunger pains, you can nevertheless snack on this to your heart's content. Snack, you say? That's supposed to be sugary and salty, right? Hmm, there are snacks to help you lose weight and snacks that pack on the pounds. Take your pick.

It could not be easier to make and the slow simmering acts to bring out flavor notes normally produced by sautéing the vegetables in butter or oil. I find that a pinch of cinnamon heightens the flavor. Use this as a base and add your favorite low calorie vegetables, such as zucchini, eggplant, parsnips and the like.

6 cups chicken stock, vegetable stock or water
1 onion, chopped
3 carrots, peeled and diced
2 stalks celery
3 cups favorite greens
3 cups summer squash, such as zucchini, patty pan or yellow zucchini, chopped
¼ head of cabbage, chopped
3 fresh tomatoes or 1 small can chopped tomatoes
3 cloves garlic
¼ cup chopped parsley
3 tablespoons fresh herbs, such as oregano, thyme, marjoram or savory
Salt and pepper to taste

In a large stockpot, put all the ingredients and bring to a boil. Reduce the heat and simmer for 1 hour or until the stock is flavorful and the vegetables are tender. Taste for seasoning.

Servings: approximately 8

CHAPTER TWENTY-TWO

Sweet Pea Soup With Mint

Because peas are higher in calories than the rest of the soups in this collection, you must limit yourself to one-half cup before a meal. But it is just so bright and refreshing, I couldn't resist including it. Not as an everyday soup, though.

1 teaspoon yogurt butter or coconut oil
1 tablespoon chicken stock
2 tablespoons green onions, coarsely chopped, white part only
1 cup fresh or frozen green peas (not canned)
1 lettuce leaf, preferably butter, but not red or it will discolor the soup
1 cup vegetable or chicken stock
1/2 cup water
Salt and pepper to taste
1 teaspoon fresh lemon juice, or more if desired
1 tablespoon chopped mint

In a medium size saucepan, melt the butter with the tablespoon of chicken stock over medium heat. Add the onions and stir over low-medium heat to allow them to sweat, about 3 minutes until they are soft. Add the peas, the remaining chicken stock, and water. Bring to a boil, then immediately reduce heat. Simmer for 5 minutes or until peas are tender and the lettuce has wilted, but do not overcook. Stir occasionally.

Do not allow the heat to get too high or the peas will discolor. They require very little cooking.

Puree the soup with an immersion blender, regular blender or in a food processor until smooth. If you use a regular blender or food processor, puree in batches and hold the lid down with a towel to prevent a soup explosion.

Stir in the lemon juice, salt and pepper to taste.

Garnish with mint before serving.

Servings: 1

CHAPTER TWENTY-THREE

Carrot, Fennel and Blood Orange Soup

This luxurious soup can make you glad you are on a diet. Delicate and full of flavor, as well as low calorie, what more can you ask for? Caution: If you are tempted to garnish the soup with some orange zest as you would with lemon zest, the blood orange rind is quite pungent, so use sparingly if at all.

1 teaspoon yogurt butter or coconut oil
1 tablespoon vegetable or chicken broth
¼ cup leek or onion, diced
Generous pinch of salt
1 medium fennel bulb, trimmed and thinly sliced; fronds reserved
1 1/2 pounds carrots, about 4 large, ends trimmed, peeled and sliced
4 to 5 cups chicken or vegetable stock
Juice of one blood orange
Salt and pepper to taste

In a medium size saucepan, melt butter and stock together over medium-low heat. Add leek and salt and cook, stirring until softened. Don't let the heat get too high or the stock will evaporate and the leek will scorch.

Add the fennel, carrots and stock and bring to a boil. Reduce the heat cover and simmer, until carrots are very tender, about 20 minutes.

With an immersion blender, a regular blender or food processor, puree the soup until smooth. If you use a regular blender or food processor, puree the soup in batches and hold down the lid with a kitchen towel or you risk the top exploding and spraying you and the kitchen with soup.

Stir in the orange juice, and season to taste with salt and pepper. Garnish with reserved fennel fronds. I don't use salt with this soup but some people like it.

Servings: 6

CHAPTER TWENTY-FOUR

Creamy Vegetable Chowder

I like to save this chowder for the weekend, when I can start it in the slow cooker and have it ready by dinnertime. If you don't use a slow cooker or crockpot, simmer the soup for 1-½ hours over low heat. If the liquid starts to evaporate, just add more chicken stock. This is a terrific soup base if you want to add beef or chicken to make a one-dish dinner. The pinch of sugar takes the bite out of the tomato and marinara sauce, but would not be needed in a meat soup.

1/2 cup chopped celery
1/2 cup sliced carrots
4 ounces vegetable juice
3 cups chicken or beef stock
1 cup favorite marinara sauce or crushed tomatoes
14-ounce package frozen mixed vegetables
2 cloves crushed garlic
1/2 teaspoon dried basil, crushed
1/2 teaspoon dried oregano, crushed

1/2 teaspoon sugar
Salt and pepper to taste.
1 bay leaf

Add the all the ingredients to the slow cooker, stir to blend, cover and cook on low for 6 hours. Remove and discard the bay leaf. With an immersion blender, regular blender or food processor, puree until smooth.

If you use a regular blender or food processor, puree the soup in batches and hold down the lid with a kitchen towel or you risk the top exploding and spraying you and the kitchen with soup. Season to taste with salt and pepper.

Servings: 6

CHAPTER TWENTY-FIVE

Spicy Cold Tomato Soup

This quick version of gazpacho is perfect for those with an overflowing tomato patch in their garden. Otherwise, seek out the fresh, sweet tomatoes from your favorite farmers market and enjoy this cooling soup on a hot day. A make ahead soup, it needs to chill before serving.

2 pounds ripe cherry tomatoes, red and yellow, stems removed and washed
4 large tomatoes, preferably heirloom, stems removed and washed
1 tablespoon chopped canned chilies
1 cup vegetable juice
2 cups vegetable or chicken stock
2 cloves of garlic or to taste, smashed and peeled
1/2 small red onion, peeled and coarsely chopped
3 tablespoons balsamic vinegar
Salt and pepper to taste
¼ cup chopped fresh basil

Place the cherry tomatoes, large tomatoes, chilies, vegetable juice and garlic in a blender or food processor.

Starting on slow power and increasing the speed gradually, puree until smooth. Be sure to hold the lid down with a kitchen towel. Add the onions and balsamic vinegar and stir well. Season to taste with salt and pepper and chill. Stir in the basil before serving.

Servings: 4-6

CHAPTER TWENTY-SIX

Cream of Mushroom Soup

Mushrooms and shallots are a favorite combo of mine, especially in this creamy soup. I used to make this with cream and brandy but find it is just as delicious stripped down to its essentials. Clean mushrooms by swishing them briefly in a bowl of cold water with a splash of white vinegar added, which removes the grit. Rinse and pat dry on paper towels.

    1 teaspoon yogurt butter or coconut oil
    1 tablespoon chicken stock
    1 pound regular white mushrooms, cleaned and quartered
    2 tablespoon minced shallots
    Generous pinch of salt
    1 tablespoon chopped fresh thyme or 1 teaspoon dried thyme
    1 1/2 – 2 cups chicken stock
    1 tablespoon lemon juice
    Salt and pepper to taste
    Minced parsley for garnish

In a medium size saucepan over medium heat, melt the butter with the chicken stock. Add the shallots, salt and stir until they are softened. Do not have the heat too high or the liquid will evaporate and scorch the shallots.

Add the mushrooms and thyme and stir briefly over moderate heat.

Add the salt, pepper and chicken stock and bring to boil. Reduce heat and simmer for 20 minutes. With an immersion blender, a regular blender or food processor, puree the soup until smooth. If you use a regular blender or food processor, puree the soup in batches and hold down the lid with a kitchen towel or you risk the top exploding and spraying you and the kitchen with soup.

Season to taste with salt, pepper and lemon juice. Thin as desired with additional chicken stock.

Serve sprinkled with a little parsley.

Servings: 4

CHAPTER TWENTY-SEVEN

Zucchini and Garlic Soup

This can be a warming winter soup, since vegetables are so widely available out of season. However, you can easily enjoy this cold in the summer. I particularly love the silky texture that can trick the palate into thinking it is rich with cream. Which, of course, it has not a drop. Be sure to cook the garlic long enough so that it loses its bite and begins to sweeten.

1 teaspoon yogurt butter or coconut oil
2 tablespoon chicken or vegetable stock
1 white onion, chopped
Generous pinch of salt
8 to 9 large cloves garlic, minced
4 medium zucchini, ends trimmed, sliced
4 cups chicken or vegetable broth
1/4 teaspoon curry powder
1/4 teaspoon ground ginger
Salt and pepper to taste

In a medium size saucepan, melt the yogurt butter or coconut oil with the stock over medium heat. Add the sliced onion, salt and garlic and simmer on medium-low heat for about 10 minutes, or until the onion is soft and translucent. Don't allow the liquid to boil or the onion and garlic will scorch.

Add the zucchini and stir. Add the stock and bring to a boil. Reduce the heat and simmer until the zucchini is tender and the garlic is soft, about 20-25 minutes.

Let cool slightly, then stir in the curry and ginger. Puree with an immersion blender, regular blender or food processor. If you use a regular blender or food processor, puree in two batches and hold the lid down with a towel to prevent a soup explosion.

Season to taste with salt and pepper.

Servings: 6

CHAPTER TWENTY-EIGHT

Roasted Red Pepper Red Soup

This soup is worth making for the color alone, a deep red from the peppers and tomatoes, and then given a touch of the sun with the orange carrots. Roasted peppers and onions can serve double duty as a snack food in my book. But in this soup they provide a deep robust flavor you would expect from onions simmered in butter. Yum-licious, if there is such a word.

Preheat oven to 425 degrees F.

4 red bell peppers, stems removed, quartered and seeded
2 onions, peeled and quartered
Cooking spray
Salt and freshly ground pepper
3 large carrots, chopped
3 large cloves garlic, crushed, skin removed
3 whole tomatoes, stems removed, quartered
6 cups chicken stock

Place the peppers and onions on a baking sheet coated with cooking spray or line the baking sheet with foil for easy cleanup. Spray the peppers and onions with cooking spray, sprinkle with salt and pepper and place in the lower third of the oven for 30 minutes.

In a medium size saucepan place the carrots, garlic and roasted vegetables. Add the tomatoes and chicken stock and bring to a boil. Immediately reduce the heat and simmer for 30-40 minutes until the carrots are tender and the soup is flavorful.

With an immersion blender, regular blender or food processor, blend the soup until smooth. If you use a regular blender or food processor, puree in batches and cover the lids with a kitchen towel and hold down to prevent the tops from exploding. Season to taste with salt and pepper.

Servings: 6

CHAPTER NINE

Curried Carrot Soup

A few drops of sesame oil deepens the rich Asian flavors without adding too many calories.

1 teaspoon yogurt butter or coconut oil
2 tablespoons chicken stock
1 medium onion, chopped
Generous pinch of salt
1 1/2 pounds packaged mini carrots
4-5 cups chicken stock
1 tablespoon mild curry paste or 1 tablespoons curry powder, or to taste
1 nickel size coin of fresh ginger, or to taste
1/4 to 1/2 teaspoon ground cayenne pepper
3-4 drops of Asian sesame oil, or to taste.
Salt and pepper to taste
6 blades fresh chives, cut into 1-inch pieces

In a medium saucepan over medium high heat, melt the yogurt or coconut oil and chicken stock together. Add the onion and salt and simmer for 5 minutes or until the onion begins to soften. Add 4 cups of the chicken stock, the carrots, curry, ginger and cayenne bring to a boil. Reduce the heat and simmer over medium heat until the carrots are very tender, about 20 minutes.

With an immersion blender, regular blender or food processor, puree the soup until smooth. If you use a regular blender or food processor, puree in batches and hold the lid down with a towel to prevent a soup explosion. Thin the soup if necessary with more stock. Add the sesame oil if desired and salt and pepper to taste.

Servings: 6

CHAPTER THIRTY

Roasted Cauliflower Soup

I sometimes puree cooked cauliflower and serve it instead of potatoes or noodles. Here the fresh thyme adds a delicate flavor to this light but nourishing soup. Roasting the cauliflower and onions makes this a very easy soup to assemble.

 1 medium cauliflower, broken into florets
 1 small yellow onion, peeled and quartered
 Cooking spray
 Salt and pepper
 5-6 cups chicken stock
 3 stalks or fresh thyme or 1 teaspoon dried
 2 bay leaves
 Fresh lemon juice

Preheat the oven to 375 degrees F.

Place the cauliflower and onion on a baking sheet covered with a light film of cooking spray or a piece of foil for easy cleanup. Coat the onion and cauliflower with the cooking spray as well and season lightly with salt and pepper. Roast in the preheated oven for 20-25 minutes until the onions begin to soften and the cauliflower starts to brown. They don't have to be thoroughly cooked as they will continue cooking in the soup.

Place the chicken stock in a medium size saucepan and add the cauliflower, onions, thyme and bay leaves. Bring to a boil over high heat, then immediately reduce the heat to a simmer. Cook for 20 minutes or until the cauliflower and onions are tender. Season to taste with salt and pepper.

Discard the bay leaves and thyme stalks. With an immersion blender, regular blender or food processor, puree the soup until smooth. Process in batches if you use a regular blender or food processer and be sure to hold the lid down with a kitchen towel so it doesn't fly off and spray you with hot soup. If you used dried thyme, you will, of course, likely notice small dark specks.

Season to taste with salt and pepper and a squirt of fresh lemon juice before serving.

Servings: 4-6

CHAPTER THIRTY-ONE

Cream of Eggplant and Tomato Soup

This reminds me so much of ratatouille, the Mediterranean vegetable stew that I adore. I could eat this every day. Again, this is a soup made easy by roasting, especially the eggplants. The skin then quickly slides off, saving you the chore of peeling them.

3 medium tomatoes, halved
1 large eggplant, whole and unpeeled
1 small onion, halved
Cooking spray
6 large garlic cloves, smashed
1 tablespoon chopped fresh thyme or 1 teaspoon dried
A pinch of red pepper flakes, or to taste
4 cups chicken stock or vegetable stock
Preheat oven to 400°F.

Place the tomatoes, eggplant, and onion on a large baking sheet covered with a light film of cooking spray or aluminum foil for easy cleanup. Spray the vegetables with cooking spray as well and season lightly with salt and pepper. Roast in the oven for 30 minutes or until tender.

When cool enough to handle, slice the eggplant in half and scoop out the pulp. Discard the skin and place the pulp with the other vegetables in a medium size saucepan. Add the thyme, chicken stock and red pepper flakes if you are using them. Bring to a boil, then reduce the heat and simmer for 25 minutes or until everything is tender and the stock is richly flavored.

With an immersion blender, regular blender or food processer, puree the soup until smooth. If you use a regular blender or food processor, puree in batches with a kitchen towel held firmly over the lid to prevent a Mt. Vesuvius erupting in your kitchen. Season to taste with salt and pepper before serving.

Servings: 4-6

CHAPTER THIRTY-TWO

Spicy Asparagus Soup

I don't know about you, but I don't equate elegant, sedate asparagus with hot sauce. Yet, a squirt of lemon and a dash of Tabasco bring this creamy soup to life. On its own, asparagus soup without cream or other thickening is pretty thin. So I've added spinach to provide texture and more of those flavorful antioxidants. How far up the tip should you peel the asparagus? I remove the tough outer skin and when I reach the tender part I stop.

    1 teaspoon yogurt butter or coconut oil
    1 tablespoon chicken stock
    1 large shallot, peeled and chopped
    Generous pinch of salt
    1 pound asparagus, hard ends peeled and sliced
    1 cup loosely packed baby spinach leaves
    4 cups chicken stock
    Dash of Tabasco sauce, to taste
    Salt and pepper to taste
    1 tablespoon fresh lemon juice, to taste

In a medium saucepan, melt the yogurt butter or coconut oil and salt with the stock over medium heat. Add the shallot and salt and stir until it begins to soften, 3-4 minutes.

Add the asparagus and chicken stock and bring to a boil, stirring constantly. Reduce the heat and add the Tabasco sauce, salt and pepper to taste.

Reduce heat to a simmer; continue cooking until asparagus is tender, about 10-12 minutes. Do not overcook or the asparagus will darken, which won't ruin the taste but the color is less appetizing than bright green when cooked just until done.

Add the spinach and stir until wilted, about 1 minute or so.

With an immersion blender, regular blender or food processer, puree the soup until smooth. If you use a regular blender or food processor, puree in batches and hold the lid down with a towel to prevent a soup explosion. Season to taste with salt, pepper and lemon juice before serving.

Yield 4 servings

CHAPTER THIRTY-THREE

Leek and Spinach Soup

I'm not sure if this is leek with spinach soup or spinach with leek. Both vegetables are delicious on their own, but sublime when matched in this simple soup. I add a touch of nutmeg which, when I was learning to cook, was the only way to serve spinach. That garnish has gone out of style, it seems. I rarely see it in spinach recipes, so I have decided to revive it here. It works so well with the leeks. To clean the leeks (they are very sandy), split them length wise to the center and hold them under running water, peeling them back as you would a deck of cards. You may have to use your fingers to remove some of the grit. Then swish them in a bowl of cold water with a splash of white vinegar added and rinse under cold water before slicing.

1 teaspoon yogurt butter or coconut oil
1 tablespoon chicken stock
4 cups chopped leeks

Generous pinch of salt
6 cups chicken stock
1 teaspoon dried thyme
¼ teaspoon ground nutmeg
2/3 cup tightly packed fresh spinach leaves

In a medium size saucepan, melt the yogurt butter or coconut oil with the chicken stock over medium heat. Add the leeks and salt and cook just until they begin to soften, about 5 minutes. Stir frequently. Add the chicken stock and thyme nutmeg and raise the heat to a boil. Reduce the heat and simmer until the leeks are tender, 15-20 minutes.

Add the spinach and stir until the leaves wilt, 1 minute or so.

With an immersion blender, regular blender or food processor, puree the soup until smooth. If you use a regular blender or food processor, puree in batches and hold the lid down with a towel to prevent a soup explosion. Season with nutmeg, salt and pepper to taste before serving.

Servings: 4

CHAPTER THIRTY-FOUR

Broccoli, Celery and Spinach Soup with Garlic

I think of this as the Jolly Green Giant soup, as long as it does not overcook and turn dark. You want the broccoli tender but not mushy. So good with a spritz of lemon that compliments the garlic.

1 teaspoon yogurt butter or coconut oil
2-3 tablespoons chicken stock
Generous pinch of salt
1 medium onion, chopped
4 stalks celery, diced
4 garlic cloves, minced
2 pounds broccoli, florets separated, stems chopped
6 cups chicken stock
Salt and freshly ground pepper to taste
2/3 ounces baby spinach
Fresh lemon juice

In a medium size saucepan, melt the yogurt butter or coconut oil with the chicken stock over medium heat. Add the salt, onion, celery and garlic and stir over low heat until the onion starts to soften. Do not have the heat high or the liquid will evaporate. Because of the quantity of onion and celery, they will scorch, though the pinch of salt will help draw the liquid out of the vegetables to prevent this. They don't have to cook through, just sauté a little to release their flavor.

Add the broccoli and stock and bring to a boil. Reduce the heat and simmer for 25-30 minutes until the broccoli and onion are tender. Do not cover the pot or the broccoli will discolor. Add the spinach and stir until wilted.

With an immersion blender, regular blender or food processor, puree until smooth. If you use a regular blender or food processor, puree in batches and hold the lid down with a towel to prevent a soup explosion. Season to taste with salt and pepper and a squeeze of lemon before serving.

Servings: 6

I stuffed a shirt or two into my old carpet-bag, tucked it under my arm, and started for Cape Horn and the Pacific. Quitting the good city of old Manhatto, I duly arrived in New Bedford. It was a Saturday night in December. Much was I disappointed upon learning that the little packet for Nantucket had already sailed, and that no way of reaching that place would offer, till the following Monday.

CHAPTER THIRTY-FIVE

Rutabaga and Carrot Soup

I have to give my mother credit for this soup, though she never tasted it. But when I was growing up, mashed carrots and rutabagas were a stable at holiday dinners. I came to love the dish, though I've never seen it on anyone's table or in a cookbook. In researching vegetables appropriate for the Soup Diet, I brushed aside my first thought of blending rutabaga into a soup because I assumed, as a root vegetable that it would too caloric. Out of curiosity, I looked it up and to my delighted surprise learned that it is highly nutritious and low calorie to boot. I hope you enjoy this treat from my childhood. If you cannot find rutabaga, substitute turnips or parsnips.

1 cup rutabaga, peeled and chopped (the remainder can be boiled or roasted)
4 carrots, peeled and chopped
½ small onion, peeled and coarsely chopped

1 clove garlic, crushed and skin removed
5 cups chicken stock
Salt and pepper to taste

Place all the ingredients in a medium size saucepan and bring to a boil. Reduce the heat and simmer for 25-30 minutes or until the vegetables are very tender.

With an immersion blender, regular blender or food processor, puree the soup until smooth. If you use a regular blender or food processor, puree in batches and hold the lid down with a towel to prevent a soup explosion.

Season to taste with salt and pepper before serving.

6 servings

CHAPTER THIRTY-SIX

Roasted Red Beet and Orange Soup

Beets and oranges go together like, well, beets and orange. Harvard beets, beet and orange salad with goat cheese— trending right now, and here, beet and orange soup. They really do compliment each other in many ways, especially if you use blood oranges to give that deep coppery glow to the soup. When blood oranges are out of season, during the spring and summer months, use regular juicy oranges such as Valencia. Sometimes I add a little ginger to spice it up.

2 large beets
1 yellow onion, peeled and halved
Cooking spray
5 cups chicken stock
1 large garlic clove, crushed
1 cup freshly squeezed blood orange juice
Salt and pepper to taste

Preheat oven to 425 F.

Spray the beets with a light film of cooking spray and wrap in foil.

Spray the onion with a light film of cooking spray.

Place the beets and onion on a baking sheet covered with foil for easy cleanup. Place in the oven for 45 minutes or until the beets are tender. Remove the onions after 30 minutes or so when they are tender and set aside until the beets are done.

Allow the beets to cool until you can handle them, then slip off the skins and chop them coarsely.

Place the beets and onion in a medium size saucepan. Add the chicken stock and garlic. Raise the heat to a boil, then reduce to a simmer Stirring frequently, cook for 15 minutes or until the garlic is tender and the soup is flavorful.

With an immersion blender, regular blender or food processor, puree the soup until smooth. If you use a regular blender or food processor, puree in batches and hold the lid down with a towel to prevent a soup explosion. Add the blood orange juice and purée until smooth. Season to taste with salt and pepper before serving.

Servings: Approximately 6

CHAPTER THIRTY-SEVEN

Lacinato Kale and Leek Soup

Kale has taken the health food crowd by storm. Prized for its dense concentration of vitamins and minerals, it is the Italian kale, or Lacinato, that takes the gold medal for flavor. Lacinato is just as healthy but milder and is made cream and rich with leeks in this yummy soup. I like the addition of a bit of balsamic vinegar with the bold flavor of kale, but use or not as you desire.

1 teaspoon yogurt butter or coconut oil
1 tablespoon chicken stock
1 leek, white part only, cleaned and diced
2 cloves garlic, smashed and skin removed
1 small bunch of Lacinato kale
3 cups chicken stock
Salt and pepper to taste
1 tablespoon balsamic vinegar, white optional

In a medium size saucepan, melt the yogurt butter or coconut oil with the chicken stock over medium heat. Add the leek and garlic and stir over low-medium heat for 3-5 minutes or until the leek has softened.

Add the kale and chicken stock and bring to a boil. Reduce the heat and simmer over medium heat for 20 minutes or until the kale and leeks are tender.

With an immersion blender, regular blender or food processor, puree the soup until smooth. Season to taste with salt and pepper. Add the balsamic vinegar, a little at a time, tasting as you go until it has the desired piquancy. Taste and add salt or pepper as desired before serving.

Servings: 4

CHAPTER THIRTY-EIGHT

Herbal Summer Squash Soup

The bounty of summer in a bowl.

1 teaspoon yogurt butter or coconut oil
2 tablespoons chicken stock
1 medium onion
4 cloves garlic, crushed
Generous pinch of salt
1 teaspoon cumin seeds
1 1/2 pounds summer squash, zucchini, yellow, patty pan or a mix, coarsely chopped
3-4 cups chicken stock
1 tablespoon mixed, fresh herbs, such as marjoram, thyme and basil, chopped
Salt and pepper, to taste

In a medium saucepan, melt the yogurt butter or coconut oil with the chicken stock over medium heat. Add the garlic, onion and salt and cook, stirring frequently until softened. Don't have the heat too high or the liquid will evaporate and the vegetables will scorch. Add the cumin seeds and cook, stirring often, until just fragrant, about a minute or two. Add squash and chicken stock and bring to a boil. Reduce the heat and simmer for 15 minutes or until the vegetables are tender.

Remove from heat and stir in the herbs. With an immersion blender, regular blender or food processor, puree the soup until smooth, holding the lid down with a towel to prevent a soup explosion. Season to taste with salt and pepper before serving.

Servings: 5-6

CHAPTER THIRTY-NINE

Creamy, Lemony Spinach Soup

The lemon in this soup makes it extremely fresh and bright, just the thing to take the edge off your appetite. If you would like a little more pucker power, grate some lemon zest, the thin part of the rind into the soup as a garnish.

1 teaspoon yogurt butter or coconut oil
2 tablespoons chicken stock
Generous pinch of salt
2 medium shallots, peeled and diced
1 large clove garlic, crushed
4 cups chicken stock
8 ounce bag of prewashed baby spinach
1 small pinch cayenne pepper
1 pinch fresh ground nutmeg
Juice of one lemon
Salt and pepper to taste

In a medium saucepan, melt the yogurt butter or coconut oil with the chicken stock over medium heat. Add the salt, shallots and garlic and stir over medium low heat until softened, about 3-4 minutes.

Add the chicken stock, spinach, cayenne and nutmeg. Bring to a boil, then reduce the heat to a simmer. Cook over gentle heat until the shallots and garlic are softened and cooked through and the spinach is wilted, about 5-8 minutes. Don't overcook or the spinach will darken.

With an immersion blender, regular blender or food processor, puree the soup, holding the lid down with a towel to prevent a soup explosion. Add the lemon and salt and pepper to taste. Stir well before serving

Servings: 4

CHAPTER FORTY

Cold Cucumber Herb Soup

This is a refreshing soup on a hot day, made especially enjoyable if you can pluck the herbs from your own garden.

6 small or 4 medium cucumbers, peeled and seeded
1 stalk of celery
½ apple
1/4 cup fresh mint
1/4 cup fresh basil
½ cup ice water
Salt and pepper to taste

Combine all ingredients in a blender and puree until smooth. Chill until ready to serve, and garnish with mint or basil leaves.

Servings: 2

CHAPTER FORTY-ONE

Smoothies

Smoothies are as good as soup for filling you up and staving off hunger pangs. A small glass of a fruit or green smoothie before a meal will also help you reduce the total calories you consume. After all, a smoothie is really a cold soup. However, you cannot use protein powder, yogurt, ice cream, milk, bananas or other high calorie ingredients. Use greens, berries, celery apples, oranges, red peppers, summer squash and steamed broccoli (unless you like raw broccoli), and add ice and water to thin it out.

Feel free to put lower calorie fruit into your Soup Diet smoothies, but don't use fruit exclusively because of the high sugar content. Use berries, citrus fruits, apples, melon, pears or grapes blended with greens, carrots, celery and other low calorie vegetables. Enjoy a half to one cup of your favorite smoothie half an hour before mealtime and put the remainder in the refrigerator for an evening snack.

This is an ideal way to sneak in those important fruits and vegetables without having to cook them.

The ideal blender for smoothies, in fact for any type of pureeing and blending, is the Vitamix or Blendtec brands. You may have seen the Blendtec videos on YouTube proclaiming they will blend anything, even your iPhone. And they will. Vitamix is a similarly powerful mixer. You do not need to peel carrots and you can add the antioxidant-rich stems of strawberries.

However, these high-powered appliances are three and four times the price of standard blenders you may have for making margaritas or pureeing soup. If you can afford them, I urge you to get one. I have the Blendtec and absolutely love it. When you juice vegetables you get all the pulp, which is very healthful, and no messy juicer to clean. But use whatever blender you have and can afford. With low power blenders you may find that the smoothies do not puree as well as the soups for those recipes that contain hard vegetables, such as carrots and celery. Try a food processor.

You can also buy canned celery, carrot and other juices and blend them with fruits that won't wreak havoc with a lower end blender. Just make sure you read the labels and don't buy products with additives and pass on the high calories juices.

Here are ten smoothies to send you on your flat belly way.

CHAPTER FORTY-TWO

Carrot, Apple, and Celery Smoothie

This is my morning smoothie, because I always have these ingredients on hand. I used to eat fruit for breakfast, but find now I prefer a smoothie.

1 carrot, ends trimmed
1 apple, cored
1 large stalk of celery
3 large sprigs of parsley
1 cup of ice water

Place all ingredients except the ice water in a high-powered blender or juicer and puree. Add the ice water and stir before serving.

CHAPTER FORTY-THREE

Blackberries, Apple, Blueberry Green Tea and Ginger Smoothie

Green tea is regarded by many as a superfood, health booster and weight loss aid. In China, people drinking green tea from a thermos all day is as common as coffee in paper cups elsewhere. I visited the tea plantation that produces Emperor tea outside of Beijing. The story goes that in times past, only the Emperor and his family were allowed to drink this tea because of its high quality. Today they still roast the leaves by hand. Having paid a King's ransom for a box of Emperor's tea when I visited the plantation, I can attest to its superior taste. For this smoothie, however, any of the flavored green teas available in your supermarket will work with the same health-giving properties. I specifically developed this smoothie to take advantage of the weight loss power of green tea. I like the blueberry, however, many flavors are available.

½ cup blackberries
1 small apple, cored
1 cup iced Blueberry Green Tea
¼ inch coin of fresh ginger

Place the blackberries, apple Blueberry green tea and ginger in a blender and puree until smooth.

Servings: 1

CHAPTER FORTY-FOUR

Grapes, Zucchini, Greens, and Celery Smoothie

Resveratrol, found in the skin of red grapes, is a chemical reputed to extend the human lifespan. Research on that score is ongoing, but perhaps, that is why red wine is considered such a healthy beverage. Here we use the grapes in a red and green smoothie. And while it is extremely good for you, and will help you control hunger pangs, I make no claims that you will live as long as Methuselah if you drink it.

1 dozen red or green grapes, stems removed
1 small zucchini, ends trimmed
1 cup spinach, arugula, kale or other greens
1 stalk celery
1 cup ice water
Place all the ingredients in a blender and puree until smooth.
Servings: 2

CHAPTER FORTY-FIVE

Apple, Melon and Greens Smoothie

Use any melon, cantaloupe, Honeydew, even watermelon in this sweet anti-oxidant-rich drink.

1 apple
1 medium wedge of cantaloupe or other melon, seeds removed
1 cup of favorite greens, such as red lettuce, spinach or kale
1 tablespoon chopped mint
1 cup ice water

Place all the ingredients in a blender and puree until smooth.

Servings: 1

CHAPTER FORTY-SIX

Berries, Red Pepper, Celery, and Parsley Smoothie

Don't forget the superfood properties of herbs. Parsley adds a bracing note to this smoothie, made sweet from the berries and pepper. The taste of red pepper predominates, which is good news to me, but you could double the strawberries and use ¾ of the pepper if you like.

¼ cup strawberries or blackberries
1 red pepper, quartered, stem and seeds discarded
1 large stalk of celery
¼ cup parsley
1/2 cup ice cold water

Place all the ingredients in a blender and puree until smooth.

Servings: 1

CHAPTER FORTY-SEVEN

Watermelon, Celery, Cucumber, and Greens Smoothie

One of the reasons watermelon is such a desirable treat during the hot summer is because it contains a great deal of water and helps keep you hydrated. Good any time of year, but think of it when the temperature climbs or you are dehydrated from an illness or workout session.

    1 cup watermelon chunks, seeds removed
    1 large stalk of celery
    1 half cucumber, peeled and seeded
    1 cup red lettuce or arugula
    1 cup green tea, any flavor

Place all the ingredients in a blender and puree until smooth.

Servings: 1

CHAPTER FORTY-EIGHT

Grapefruit, Orange, Strawberry and Red Pepper Smoothie

We are in the habit of removing the stems from strawberries when we eat them whole or in desserts. However, those little leaves contain vitamins and antioxidants. If you have a strong enough blender you can put the strawberries in whole and you won't know the difference.

Pulp of 1 small grapefruit, seeds removed
Pulp of 1 orange, seeds removed
1 cup of strawberries, washed and stems removed (optional)
1 small red pepper, quartered and seeded
1 cup ice water

Place all the ingredients in a blender and puree until smooth.

Servings: 1

CHAPTER FORTY-NINE

Vegetable Juice, Celery, Apple, and Basil Smoothie

Canned vegetable juice is an ideal hunger suppressor if you are on the run and can't find or make a smoothie or soup. Here it is mixed with vegetables, apples and herbs to make an especially healthful drink.

4 ounces canned vegetable juice
1 stalk of celery
1 carrot
½ apple, cored, unpeeled
2 tablespoons fresh basil

Place all the ingredients in a blender and puree until smooth.

Servings: 1

CHAPTER FIFTY

Green Tea, Apple, Spinach, and Carrot Smoothie

Green tea appears again in this smoothie, but you can use a flavored tea or plain because the apple, spinach and carrots make the smoothie tasty on its own.

8 ounces green tea
½ apple, cored, unpeeled
1½ cup baby spinach leaves
6 mini carrots

Place all the ingredients in a blender and puree until smooth.

Servings: 1

CHAPTER FIFTY-ONE

Apple Cinnamon Smoothie

Cinnamon adds not just flavor to this drink, but it has many nutritional components that qualify it as a superfood, one of the vitamin and mineral-packed powerhouses that are finally getting attention.

1 pear, cored and sliced, not peeled
1 apple, cored and sliced
1 cup fresh spinach
1/4 teaspoon ground cinnamon or nutmeg
1/2 cup ice

Place all ingredients except the ice in the blender jar and puree until smooth. Taste for seasoning, adding more cinnamon or nutmeg. Add the ice and blend until the ice is crushed and the smoothie is thick.

Servings: 2

Bon Appetit and Good Health

Give The Book A Thumbs Up

Most cooks agree that a cookbook is worth the price if you find even one recipe that becomes a favorite. I hope you will find many recipes that will please you and make your kitchen life easier.

Positive reviews are the lifeblood of writers. Please go to this website:

http://www.amazon.com/dp/B00BRRZQC2 and leave a positive review for The Soup Diet Cookbook on Amazon and Like it on Facebook.

Help me spread the word about my health and wellness books by telling your friends and gifting them to your loved ones.

Many thanks for your interest in my book. If I can answer any questions for you, please contact me at cookhealthyinahurry@gmail.com

Medical Disclaimer

The information in this book is for educational purposes only. It is not meant to provide or replace medical advice you may have received. If you are concerned about a medical or health issue, contact your health care provider immediately. If you are pregnant, have a major health issue, are under 18 or over 65, do not embark on any dietary changes without consulting your physician or other health care provider.

The dietary suggestions in this book are not meant to cure an illness. Your first line of defense in promoting good health is always a consultation with your health care provider. Feel free to discuss this book with your doctor or nutritionist and tailor the book and recipes to your own needs.

About Me

I have been writing about health, wellness, food and cooking for four decades. My publishing credits include writing two heart-healthy cookbooks with Stanford University cardiologist, John S. Schroeder, M.D. My work has appeared in Gourmet, Bon Appétit, Self Magazine and Men's Fitness, among other magazines. I have written many articles and online columns and have made numerous public cooking demonstrations as well as radio and TV appearances. For many years I ran my own cooking school and did menu consulting for restaurants.

Please read my author page available on the website below for more information about me and my upcoming books and activities.

https://www.amazon.com/author/helencassidypage

My Other Books

My first book in this series, How To Cook Healthy In A Hurry, was a Kindle Best Seller almost from its launch. It offers the cook 50 delicious recipes that require less than 30 minutes in the kitchen and are packed with flavor and nutrition. I even have a testimonial from a 7 year old that his favorite dinner is from this cookbook.

Following on the success of the first How To book, I launched Volume 2. It, too, quickly became a best seller.

I launched the second in my How To Cook Healthy In A Hurry series, The Healthy Husband Cookbook. We have to do something about the typical western diet: it is killing the men we love. Whether you have a husband, are a husband or know a husband, this book is for you. Containing 35 healthy but delectable recipes that appeal to male tastes, this book will help you enjoy sumptuous meals while helping to keep you and your loved one as healthy as possible.

I also want to thank Jackie Johnson, author of Twelve Best Herbs For Flavor, for her advice on using herbs in these recipes.

Free Gift

And last, don't forget to pick up your free gift at:

http://www.helencassidypage.com/how-to-cook-healthy-in-a-hurry-bonus/

And please like and follow How To Cook Healthy In A Hurry on Facebook at:

https://www.facebook.com/HowToCookHealthyInAHurry

Happy eating and best wishes for a lifetime of good health.

Copyright Information